TEA AND CAKE

TEA AND CAKE

Illustrations by Emma Block

hardie grant books

MELBOURNE · LONDON

CONTENTS

one lump
or two?

INTRODUCTION

A tea party is suitable for all different types of celebrations, from birthdays to hen parties and baby showers, or just because you fancy the idea of being a lady who lunches. The food is all prepared before your guests arrive, so the only taxing thing left for you to do is to pour the tea. How utterly brilliant!

Your teatime menu can be as lazy or as tricky as you like. Want to dazzle with your baking skills? Make everything from scratch and pray that someone asks where you learnt your pastry wrangling skills. More interested in spending time dolling up yours truly than messing around making teeny-weeny quiches and tarts? Then defrost that roll of pastry from the back of the freezer, think of some inventive sandwich fillings and book in that blow-dry: there's no doubt you deserve it. Remember, the best part of every food soiree is the sharing.

So dust off your pinny, stick on the kettle, and get ready to grease some tins: it's time to start baking.

P IS FOR PLANNING

Ladies, there's only one thing that will ensure your tea soiree goes off without a hitch, and that's if you plan your party within an inch of its life. A last-minute dash to the supermarket for ready-made soggy sandwiches (perish the thought) and a boxed Victoria Sponge that has a use-by date ten years from now, is simply not acceptable. So what's a gal to do?

<u>Select the type of soiree:</u> Is it to be a cream, afternoon or high tea? Decisions, decisions. Here's the low-down: cream tea is usually scones, jam, clotted cream and a brew, and is rather informal -- perfect for a rainy day and a chit-chat; afternoon tea is traditionally served between 3 and 5 pm, consists of savouries and sweets, and should be held in a classier fashion; afternoon tea usually happens around 6 pm and is a proper, sit-down affair with more hearty foods.

<u>Guest list:</u> There's one golden rule that all domestic goddesses stick to: never invite more people than you can comfortably cater for. This will only lead to unnecessary stress, which in turn leads to wrinkles, and no-one wants those. Less is more (and 12 should be the absolute max: you are not Nigella, after all). Think long and hard about who you would like to invite. Claudia and Samira not talking because of that 'incident' last year? Now is not the time for a reunion: hot tea BURNS, and you can still glass someone with a bone-china teacup. Choose your guests wisely. After all, you don't want the spotlight to be on two people not getting on, especially if you've spent all morning making your own damn pastry!

Invites: Your choice of invite depends on how formal you would like the afternoon to be. A written invite is the nicest to receive; a handmade one will make your guests secretly hate you (but actually want to be you); text and Facebook messages seem rather ghastly in comparison, so be it on your head! Aim to send your invites a few weeks in advance to ensure maximum attendance, and don't forget to include the date, time, venue details and dress code.

Pre-bake that cake: Giving yourself as little as possible to do on the day of the party will make your life stress-free, and allow you more time to spend on dolling yourself (and your house) up. Almost all of the cakes in this book can be made the day before. However, your dainty little finger sandwiches should be prepared just an hour before the guests arrive: a dry savoury could spell your undoing; a soggy one would mean instant fail.

Essentials: A few days before the party, make sure you have enough plates, teacups, serving platters, napkins, knives and forks and all that jazz to go around. If you were thinking plastic cutlery and paper plates would suffice you were wrong, and should seriously rethink your hostess credentials. Mismatched china will give your table a certain charm, and a quirky tablecloth or a line of bunting can add some class. What if you don't have a tablecloth? Host it anyway!

Tea selection: Hopefully you own at least one teapot, or things could get a bit tricky. For types of tea, stick to the classics like English Breakfast, Irish Breakfast and Earl Grey and you can't go wrong. It would be nice to have more than one type on offer, but delicious food will cancel out the lack of choice. Be sure to keep the kettle on the boil throughout the day to ensure that parched nerves are constantly rejuvinated.

Menu: Your menu should be light yet filling, savoury as well as sweet. When in doubt, make a tad extra: you don't want your guests going hungry. And check with everyone beforehand to see if they have any food allergies or special diets: a gluten-intolerant vegan with a nut allergy could spoil the fun if you are not totally prepared!

Playlist: There's no better way to create a party atmosphere than pumping out some of your favourite tunes. You could just plug in your iPod and hit random, but we all know this will be the moment when the explicit Lil' Kim track or that dreary Leonard Cohen number rears its ugly head and kills the vibe (or changes the tone of the party...). To avert disaster, why not create a tea-sipping playlist (or even two)?

MAKING THE PERFECT CUPPA

Ladies, the most important part of any tea soiree, from tea for two to refreshments for a gaggle of cackling hens, is perfecting the brew. Make it weak and it will taste like a cup of dishwater; too strong and you'll be using it to remove wallpaper later in the day. Follow the steps below to make the perfect brew.

1. Don't even think of making a monobrew in a ghastly cup. Use a teapot, preferably ceramic, and warm it with some boiling water.

2. Once the pot is warm, add your tea. Here's your new mantra: loose leaves make the best teas. Place one rounded teaspoon of tea per cup into the pot. (The tea gods will not hate you if you only have bags, but under no circumstance rip the bag open – it's just not the same!)

3. Take the pot to the kettle as it is boiling, pour the water onto the leaves and stir.

4. Leave it to brew for around three minutes but don't wander off to do the vacuuming! Stewed tea is most unpleasant, and you want the tea to be piping hot.

5. A tea and saucer is the most elegant way to take your tea. Pour some milk into the teacup followed by the tea, and aim for a colour of brew that is rich and attractive, or in keeping with your guest's requirements.

6. Some guests may like to add sugar to their tea. This is looked down upon by many serious tea drinkers, but try not to judge them – a good hostess is most certainly an open-minded one!

7. To avoid vulgar slurping, drink your tea at a leisurely pace, accompanied with delicious cakes and treats.

Why not ask your guests how they like their tea before you pour?
Overleaf is a guide to specific strengths, for fussy drinkers.

TEA STRENGTH: A GUIDE FOR THE HOSTESS

The strength a tea drinker likes their brew is totally down to personal taste, and one person's stewed nightmare is another's nectar of the gods. Let your guests peruse the chart below and allow them to pick their personal strength. Keep in mind that Early Grey will brew to a light golden colour, whereas teas like English and Irish Breakfast will be a slightly darker and redder hue.

Classic Brew

<u>Brewing time:</u> 2–4 minutes for this most popular of brews, with a bout 10 ml of milk

Stewed / Wallpaper Stripper

<u>Brewing time:</u> 4–6 minutes or longer with a hint of milk

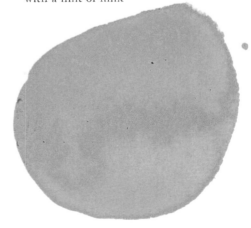

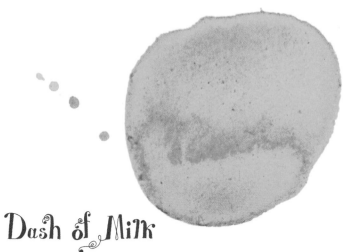

Straight-up Tea

<u>Brewing time:</u> 2–4 minutes, with a dash of water to cool it down

Dash of Milk

<u>Brewing time:</u> 2–4 minutes, with a thimble-sized shot of milk

Dirty Dishwater

<u>Brewing time:</u> 2 minutes or under with a generous amount of milk

Weak and Milky

<u>Brewing time:</u> the bag should go in and out and copious amounts of milk added

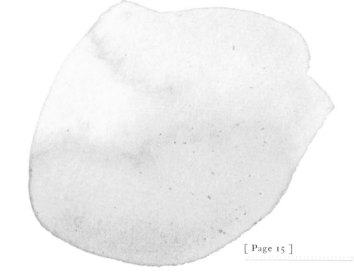

CHAPTER 1:
SANDWICHES AND SAVOURIES

WILD MUSHROOM
TARTLETS

· 10 g (⅔ oz) dried porcini mushrooms
· 2 tbsp olive oil
· 1 onion, finely diced
· 250 g (9 oz) wild mushrooms, sliced
· 2 garlic cloves, crushed
· 80 ml (2 ½ fl oz/⅓ cup) white wine
· 2 tbsp chopped flat-leaf (Italian)
parsley or basil
· sea salt and freshly ground black pepper
· 35 savoury tart shells
· fresh flat-leaf (Italian) parsley leaves,
for garnish

MAKES 30–35

❋ Pour 250 ml (9 fl oz/1 cup) boiling water over the porcini mushrooms and leave for 20 minutes. Drain, reserving the porcini and soaking liquid.

❋ Heat the oil in a saucepan over medium–high heat, add the onion and cook for 3–4 minutes or until softened and translucent. Add the wild mushrooms and cook, stirring often, for 4–5 minutes or until softened. Add the garlic and porcini and cook for 1–2 minutes or until fragrant. Add the wine and cook until reduced by half. Add the reserved liquid and bring to the boil. Reduce the heat and simmer for 10–15 minutes or until all the liquid has evaporated. Add the chopped parsley and season with salt and pepper.

❋ Spoon the hot mushroom mixture into the tart shells. Garnish with the parsley leaves.

BRIOCHE WITH
SCRAMBLED EGGS AND
SALMON CAVIAR

- 3 eggs
- 2 tbsp pouring (single) cream
- sea salt and freshly ground
- black pepper
- 40 g (1 ½ oz) butter
- 50 g (1 ¾ oz) salmon caviar (roe)
- snipped chives, for garnish

BRIOCHE DOUGH
- 2 x 7 g (½ oz) sachets dried yeast
- 1 tsp caster (superfine) sugar
- 200 g (7 oz/1 ⅓ cup) plain
  (all-purpose) flour, sifted
- 1 tsp salt
- 2 eggs, lightly beaten
- 60 g (2 ¼ oz) unsalted
  butter, melted

MAKES 25–30

* To make the dough, combine the yeast, sugar and 2 tablespoons warm water in a small bowl and leave in a warm place for 5–10 minutes or until frothy.

* Place the flour and salt in the bowl of an electric mixer fitted with a dough hook and make a well in the centre. Add the yeast mixture, egg and butter and mix on low speed to combine. Knead for 6–8 minutes or until smooth and no longer sticky. Transfer to a floured bowl, cover with a kitchen towel and leave in a warm place for 1–2 hours or until doubled in size.

* Preheat oven to 190°C (375°F/Gas 5). Line 2 baking trays with baking paper. Knock back the dough and knead on a floured surface for 1–2 minutes. Roll pieces of dough into 2 cm (3/4 inch) balls and place on the trays. Flatten each slightly, cover with a kitchen towel and leave in a warm place for 20 minutes or until doubled in size. Bake for 10–15 minutes or until golden and the bottoms sound hollow when tapped.

* To make the scrambled eggs, whisk the eggs and cream together and season with salt and pepper. Heat a heavy-based frying pan over medium heat. Add the butter and egg mixture and cook, stirring frequently, for 3–4 minutes or until just set. Remove the pan from the heat; the residual heat in the pan will set the eggs.

* To serve, halve each brioche, fill with a spoonful of the scrambled eggs and 4–5 pearls of salmon caviar, and garnish with the chives.

BABY CARAMELISED ONION TARTES TARTIN

80 ml (2 ½ fl oz/⅓ cup) olive oil
3 onions, thinly sliced
2 sprigs thyme
sea salt and freshly ground black pepper
50 g (1 ¾ oz/½ cup) grated cheddar cheese

DOUGH
250 g (9 oz/1⅔ cups) self-raising (self-rising) flour
1 tsp salt
100 ml (3 ½ fl oz/⅖ cup) milk
40 g (1 ½ oz) butter, melted
1 tsp Dijon mustard
1 egg

MAKES 20

Place the oil, onion and thyme in a frying pan over low heat and cook, stirring regularly, for 20–30 minutes or until softened and caramelised. Season with salt and pepper.

Preheat oven to 180°C (350°F/Gas 4). Lightly grease two 12-hole mini-muffin trays.

Meanwhile, to make the dough, sift the flour and salt into a bowl and make a well in the centre. Whisk the milk, butter, mustard and egg together in a separate bowl. Add to the dry ingredients and mix with a fork until the dough just comes together. Knead briefly on a floured surface until smooth. Roll out to 1 cm (½ inch) thick and, using a 2 ½ cm (1 inch) round cutter, cut into 20 circles.

Place a spoonful of onion in the base of each mini-muffin hole, sprinkle with some cheese and top with a circle of dough. Bake for 10–15 minutes or until golden. Leave in tins for 3–4 minutes. To remove the tartes, cover each tray with a large plate and invert the tartes onto the plate.

CARAMELISED LEEK AND ARTICHOKE SCONES

- 40 g (1 ½ oz) butter
- ½ leek, white part only, finely diced
- 1 tbsp soft brown sugar
- 2 marinated artichoke hearts, roughly chopped
- 500 g (1 lb 2 oz/3 ⅓ cups) self-raising (self-rising) flour
- 2 tsp baking powder
- pinch of salt
- 100 g (3 ½ oz) cold unsalted butter, cubed
- 150 ml (5 fl oz/⅗ cup) buttermilk

MAKES 12

❋ Preheat oven to 220°C (425°F/Gas 7). Line a baking tray with baking paper.

❋ Heat the butter in a frying pan over medium heat, add the leek and cook for 5 minutes or until softened and golden. Add the sugar and cook for 1 minute. Stir through the artichoke and leave to cool.

❋ Place the flour, baking powder, salt and cubed butter in a food processor and pulse until the mixture resembles breadcrumbs. Add the buttermilk and 150 ml (5 fl oz/⅗ cup) cold water and pulse again until the mixture just starts to come together. Tip onto a floured surface, add the leek mixture and bring together quickly with your hands, making sure to not overwork the dough. Pat the dough out to 2 cm (¾ inch) thick. Using a 4 cm (1 ½ inch) round cutter, cut out 12 rounds and arrange so they are touching on the tray to make a neat 3 x 4 rectangle. Bake for 15 minutes or until light golden.

PEKING DUCK PANCAKES

* 200 g (7 oz) pre-cooked duck breast, skin discarded
* hoisin sauce, for spreading and dipping
* ¼ iceberg lettuce, shredded
* 1 short cucumber, cut into long, thin strips
* 1 cup coriander (cilantro) leaves

PANCAKES
* 1 egg
* 250 ml (9 fl oz/1 cup) milk
* pinch of salt
* 150 g (5 ½ oz/1 cup) plain (all-purpose) flour
* 1 tbsp snipped chives
* 30 g (1 oz) butter, melted

MAKES ABOUT 20

To make the batter, lightly whisk the egg, milk and salt together in a bowl. Whisk in the flour, a little at a time, until the batter is the consistency of thin custard. Leave to rest for 30 minutes. Strain the batter, if there are any lumps. Stir through the chives.

Heat a small, heavy-based frying pan over medium heat. Brush the pan with the butter and pour in just enough batter to form a 10 cm (4 inch) pancake. Cook for 1–2 minutes or until golden, then flip over and cook the other side until golden. Remove from the pan and repeat with the remaining batter.

Preheat oven to 180°C (350°F/Gas 4). Place the duck on a baking tray and bake for 8–10 minutes or until just heated through. Remove and thinly slice.

To serve, gently warm the pancakes in the oven. Lay the pancakes on a surface and spread with a little hoisin sauce. Place 1–2 slices of duck, some lettuce, cucumber and coriander leaves in the centre of each pancake and roll up. Serve with extra hoisin sauce for dipping.

CHEESY CHOUX
PUFFS

* 150 g (5 ¼ oz) spinach leaves
* 125 g (4 ½ oz/½ cup) ricotta
* 1 egg
* 150 g (5 ¼ oz) mashed feta
* pinch of nutmeg
* freshly ground black pepper
* 2 tbsp chopped parsley
* 6 sheets filo pastry
* 100 g (3 ½ oz) melted butter

MAKES 30

✳ Preheat oven to 180°C (350°F/Gas 4).

✳ Blanch spinach leaves in boiling water. Refresh immediately under cold running water, squeeze excess water out and chop finely. Mix spinach with ricotta, egg, feta, nutmeg, pepper and chopped parsley until smooth.

✳ Brush 1 sheet of filo pastry with melted butter, lay another sheet of filo pastry on top, brush again with butter and repeat until you have 6 sheets of filo pastry buttered together. Lay filo pastry layers in a 23 cm (9 inch) flan tin. Spoon in spinach/ricotta mix. Fold pastry ends over to enclose filling completely. Brush top with melted butter.

✳ Bake in preheated oven for 30 minutes, or until golden brown and slightly puffy.

CLASSIC TEA
SANDWICHES

It wouldn't be an afternoon tea without some finger sandwiches. Don't make them too far in advance – a soggy or dry sandwich could be your undoing! Prepare them about an hour ahead, covering them with plastic wrap and keeping them in the fridge until your guests arrive. You can really go wild with the fillings, but here are three classics to get you started.

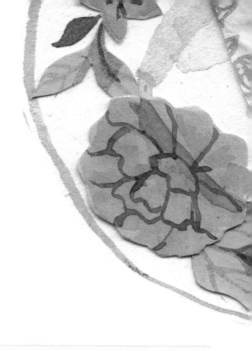

CUCUMBER SANDWICHES
WITH MINT

- ½ seedless cucumber, peeled and sliced
- ¼ cup fresh mint, finely chopped
- 60 g (2 oz) softened butter
- 60 g (2 oz/¼ cup) cream cheese
- 16 slices white bread, crusts removed
- salt

MAKES ABOUT 30

❋ Gently blot the cucumber slices to dry off any excess moisture. Blend the mint, butter and cream cheese in a mixing bowl. Evenly spread the mixture onto 8 slices of bread. Lay the cucumber slices on top of the mixture and season with salt. Top with the remaining bread, and cut the sandwiches into fingers or quarters to serve.

CREAMY EGG AND CRESS SANDWICHES

4 eggs, hardboiled and chopped
4 tbsp of the best mayonnaise you can find
salt and pepper
1 punnet of cress
16 thin slices white or wholemeal bread, crusts removed

MAKES ABOUT 30

In a large bowl, mix the chopped eggs and mayonnaise and season to taste.

Spread half of the slices of bread with the egg mixture and sprinkle some cress on top of each one, reserving some for garnishing. Top with the remaining bread, and cut the sandwiches into fingers or quarters. To serve, garnish with the remaining cress.

SMOKED SALMON SANDWICHES

- 250 g (7 ¾ oz/1 cup) soft cream cheese
- 16 slices bread (brown, white or multigrain), crusts removed
- 80 g (3 oz/½ cup) capers
- 350 g (12 ½ oz) thinly sliced smoked salmon
- juice of 1 lemon
- black pepper

MAKES ABOUT 30

✳ Spread the cream cheese onto half the slices of bread. Sprinkle with the capers. Next, arrange the smoked salmon on 8 of the bread slices and brush with lemon juice. Pepper generously. Top with the other 8 slices and cut into fingers or quarters to serve.

SMOKED SALMON BLINIS WITH CAVIAR

- *2 x 135g (5 oz) packs blinis*
- *1 tbsp horseradish*
- *200g (7 oz) crème fraiche*
- *200g (7 oz) smoked salmon, divided into small slices*
- *100g (3 ½ oz) pot salmon caviar or lump fish roe*
- *small bunch of fresh dill*

MAKES 32

❋ Wrap the blinis in foil and warm in a 200°C (400°F/Gas 6) oven for 2 minutes.

❋ Mix together the horseradish and crème fraiche and set to one side.

❋ Next, place the blinis on a platter and top each one with a dollop of the crème fraiche and horseradish mixture, a slice of smoked salmon and ¹/₂ teaspoon of the caviar or roe. Garnish with a sprig of dill.

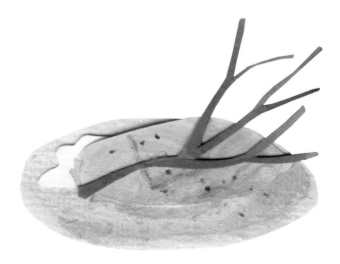

CHAPTER 2:
CAKES TO SHARE

PAVLOVA

6 egg whites
440 g (15 ½ oz/2 cups) caster (superfine) sugar
1 tsp vanilla extract
1 tbsp cornflour (corn starch)
1 ½ tsp white vinegar
250 ml (8 ½ fl oz/1 cup) whipping cream
2 kiwi fruit, peeled and sliced
200 g (7 oz/1 ½ cups) strawberries
pulp from 6 passionfruit (optional)

SERVES 6–8

Preheat oven to 180°C (350°F/Gas 4).

Beat egg whites until stiff peaks form. Add sugar, a third at a time, allowing each third to be well incorporated so that you end up with a thick glossy meringue. Fold through vanilla, cornflour and vinegar.

Either spoon onto a greased and lined 23 cm (9 inch) springform cake tin or spread in a high circle on a sheet of baking paper on a tray. Place in oven, lower temperature to 120°C (250°F/Gas ½) and bake for 45 minutes. Turn the oven off, leaving the pavlova to cool inside the oven, preferably overnight.

Place cool pavlova on a serving platter and cover with whipped cream. Decorate with the strawberries and kiwi fruit. Scoop passionfruit pulp on top for an extra fruity kick.

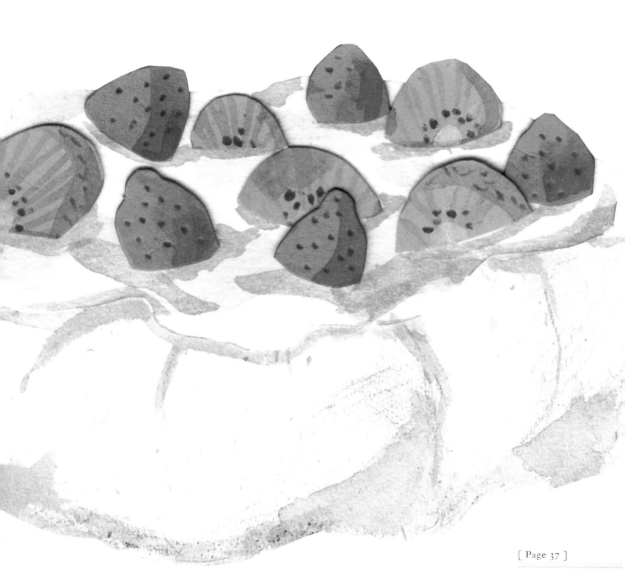

FOOL-PROOF
SPONGE CAKE

4 eggs
110 g (3 ¾ oz/½cup) caster (superfine) sugar
100 g (3 ½ oz/⅔ cup) plain (all-purpose) flour
raspberry jam as required
250 ml (8 ½ fl oz/1 cup) thickened cream, whipped
icing (confectioners') sugar to serve

SERVES 6–8

Preheat oven to 180°C (350 F/Gas 4).

Butter a 20 cm (8 inch) springform cake tin and line the sides and bottom with baking paper. Butter the paper and sprinkle it with a little plain flour to ensure that the batter won't stick.

Beat the eggs and caster sugar together until very thick and light. Carefully fold in the flour, then spoon the mix into the prepared cake tin and cook in the preheated oven for 15–20 minutes. Test the cake by inserting a skewer. If it comes out clean, the cake is ready; if it doesn't, cook for a further 2–3 minutes and test again.

Allow the cake to cool on a wire rack. When cool, remove the cake from the cake tin and peel away the baking paper. Cut the sponge in half, and spread a layer of jam and whipped cream on the bottom half of the cake. Replace the top, then sprinkle with icing sugar.

ONE-POT
CHOCOLATE CAKE

• 250 g (9 oz) soft butter
• 150 g (5 ½ oz) dark chocolate, chopped
• 220 g (7 ¾ oz/1 cup) caster (superfine) sugar
• 250 ml (8 ½ fl oz/1 cup) strong coffee
• 150 g (5 ½ oz/1 cup) plain (all-purpose) flour
• 100 g (3 ½ oz/⅔ cup) self-raising (self-rising) flour
• 50 g (2 oz/½ cup) cocoa
• 2 eggs

SERVES 6–8

✳ Preheat oven to 180°C (350°F/Gas 4).

✳ Butter a 22 cm (8 ½ inch) springform cake tin, line the sides and bottom with baking paper and butter lightly.

✳ Place the butter, chocolate, caster sugar and coffee in a large saucepan. Cook over a medium heat, stirring occasionally, until everything melts. Remove from heat and allow to cool slightly.

✳ Sift the flours and cocoa together and add to the cooled chocolate mixture, along with the eggs. Beat well until all ingredients are combined.

✳ Spoon into the prepared cake tin and bake in the preheated oven for 45 minutes. Test the cake by inserting a skewer. If it comes out clean, the cake is ready; if it doesn't, cook for a further 5 minutes and test again.

BANANA AND WALNUT CAKE

· 125 g (4 ½ oz) soft butter
· 220 g (7 ¾ oz/1 cup) caster (superfine) sugar
· 2 eggs
· 225 g (8 oz/1 ½ cups) self-raising (self-rising) flour
· 1 tsp vanilla extract
· 2 ripe bananas, mashed
· 90 g (3 ¼ oz/¾ cup) walnuts, chopped, optional

SERVES 6–8

Preheat oven to 180°C (350°F/Gas 4).

Cream butter and sugar until light and fluffy. Add eggs, one by one, incorporating well after each addition. Stir through flour, vanilla, mashed banana and walnuts.

Spoon into a greased and lined log tin 23 ½ cm × 13 ½ cm × 7 cm (9 ¼ inch × 5 inch × 2 ¾ inch) and bake in preheated oven for 20–25 minutes. Check the cake with a skewer. If it comes out clean the cake is cooked; if not, cook for a further 5–10 minutes and try again.

CARROT CAKE

- 300 g (10 ½ oz/2 cups) self-raising (self-rising) flour
- 1 tsp cinnamon
- 1 tsp mixed spice
- 4 eggs
- 330 g (11 ½ oz/1 ½ cups) caster (superfine) sugar
- 1 tsp vanilla extract
- 300 ml (10 ¼ fl oz/ 1 ¼ cups) olive or vegetable oil
- pinch of salt

- 60 g (2 oz/⅓cup) hazelnuts
- 60 g (2 oz/½ cup) walnut pieces
- 150 g (5 ½ oz/1 cup) sultanas
- 3 large grated carrots

CREAM CHEESE FROSTING
- 200 g soft cream cheese
- 110 g (½ cup) caster (superfine) sugar
- 2 tbsp lemon juice

SERVES 8–10

✳ Preheat oven to 180°C (350°F/Gas 4).

✳ Sift flour, cinnamon and mixed spice together into a large bowl. Add eggs, sugar, vanilla, oil and a pinch of salt. Mix lightly, then incorporate hazelnuts, walnuts, sultanas and grated carrots.

✳ Pour into a greased and lined 23 cm (9 inch) greased cake tin. Bake in preheated oven for 1 hour. Check the cake with a skewer. If it comes out clean, the cake is cooked; if it doesn't, cook for a further 5–10 minutes and try again. Allow to cool in tin for 15 minutes, then remove and cool on cooling rack.

✳ To make the cream cheese frosting, place all the ingredients in a food processor and blend until smooth. Spread over the cake once it has completely cooled.

VARIATION

<u>Carrot, cardamom and cashew cake</u>
Substitute ground cardamom for cinnamon, and omit mixed spices. Substitute cashews for hazelnuts and walnuts.

CHERRY CHEESECAKE

· 150 g (5 ½ oz) digestive
biscuits (graham crackers)
· 60 g (2 oz) melted butter
· 200 g (7 oz) soft cream cheese
· 110 g (3 ¾ oz/½ cup)
caster (superfine) sugar
· zest of 1 lemon
· 2 eggs
· 150 g (5 ½ oz/⅔ cup)

curd cheese or ricotta
· 200 g (7 oz) cottage cheese
· 500 g (1 lb/1 ½ oz)
pitted cherries, halved
· 80 ml (2 ¾ oz/⅓ cup) water
· 2 tbsp caster (superfine)
sugar, additional
· 1 tbsp arrowroot
· 1 tbsp cold water, additional

SERVES 6–8

Place biscuits in a food processor and whiz to form small crumbs; add melted butter and process briefly. Press biscuits into the bottom of a 22 cm (8 ½ inch) springform cake tin. Place in the refrigerator to set, for at least 20 minutes.

Preheat oven to 170°C (325°F /Gas 3).

Beat cream cheese, sugar and lemon zest until smooth. Add eggs one at a time, beating after each addition. Fold through curd and cottage cheese.

Take the cake tin and wrap the outside base with foil, using two pieces to cover the base. This prevents water seeping into the cake during cooking.

Place the cake tin in a deep baking tray. Pour in cheesecake filling over biscuit base. Pour boiling water into the baking dish to come halfway up the cake tin. Place carefully in the oven. Cook for 1 hour, or until the cake is just set, with some hint of wobble still. Allow to cool on a cooling rack before refrigerating, preferably overnight.

Place water and sugar in a saucepan and bring to the boil. Add cherries. Dissolve arrowroot in cold water and add to cherry mixture; stir until thick. Pour cherry mixture over cold cheesecake and return to the refrigerator for about 30 minutes, or until set.

VARIATION

<u>Raspberry cheesecake</u>
Substitute raspberries for cherries.

LEMON TEACAKE

- 220 g (7 ¾ oz) soft butter
- 180 g (6 ½ oz/¾ cup) caster (superfine) sugar, plus additional for sprinkling
- grated zest of 2 lemons
- 3 eggs
- 200 g (7 oz/1 ⅓ cup) self-raising (self-rising) flour
- 90 g (3 ¼ oz/⅔ cup) plain (all-purpose) flour
- 60 ml (2 fl oz/¼ cup) lemon juice

SERVES 6–8

Preheat oven to 170°C (325°F/Gas 3).

Cream butter and sugar until light and fluffy. Add lemon zest. Add eggs one at a time, allowing each to be incorporated before adding the next. Stir in flour and lemon juice and keep stirring until incorporated.

Spoon into a greased and lined loaf tin 23 ½ cm × 13 ½ cm × 7 cm (9 ¼ inch × 5 inch × 2 ¾ inch), sprinkle with additional caster sugar and bake for 1 hour. Test the cake by inserting a skewer; if it comes out clean the cake is ready. If it doesn't, cook for a further 5 minutes and test again. Allow to cool in tin before removing.

VARIATIONS

Lemon and poppyseed teacake
Add 1 tbsp poppyseeds to flour.

Orange teacake
Substitute orange zest and juice for lemon.

Cinnamon and lemon teacake
Add 1 tsp ground cinnamon to flour.

WHITE CHOCOLATE CHEESECAKE

- 150 g (5 ½ oz) chocolate-flavoured biscuits (cookies)
- 60 g (2 oz) melted butter
- 150 g (5 ½ oz) white chocolate
- 500 g (1 lb 1 ½ oz) soft cream cheese
- 150 g (5 ½ oz/²⁄₃ cup) caster (superfine) sugar
- 250 ml (8 ½ fl oz/1 cup) sour cream

SERVES 6–8

Place the biscuits in a food processor and whiz to form small crumbs. Add the melted butter and process briefly. Press the biscuit mix into the bottom of a 20 cm (8 inch) springform cake tin and place in the refrigerator to set for at least 20 minutes.

Melt the chocolate by placing it in a bowl over a saucepan of simmering water or in a microwave on low for 1–2 minutes. Beat the cream cheese and caster sugar until well softened and creamy. Add the sour cream and melted chocolate and stir into the cream cheese mixture until combined. Pour on top of the biscuit base and chill until set.

VARIATION

Dark chocolate cheesecake
Substitute dark chocolate for white chocolate.

RICOTTA TART

SWEETCRUST PASTRY SHELL
- 300 g (10 ½ oz/2 cups) plain (all-purpose) flour
- 150 g (5 ¼ oz) soft butter, diced
- pinch of salt
- 1 egg
- 55 g (2 oz/¼ cup) caster (superfine) sugar
- plain (all-purpose) flour for dusting
- 250 g (9 oz/1 cup) ricotta

- 110 g (3 ¾ oz/½ cup) caster (superfine) sugar
- 3 eggs
- 1 tsp vanilla extract
- 125 ml (4 ½ fl oz/½ cup) cream
- 2 tbsp plain (all-purpose) flour
- grated zest of 1 lemon
- 2 tbsp lemon juice
- ground cinnamon

SERVES 8

To make the pastry dough, place the flour, butter and salt in a bowl and rub together until the mixture resembles fine breadcrumbs. Break the egg into a separate bowl, add caster sugar and mix lightly. Add to the flour mixture and mix until the pastry comes together. Wrap in plastic wrap and chill for 30 minutes.

Preheat oven to 180°C (350°F/Gas 4).

Roll the pastry on a lightly floured board to 3 mm thickness. Line a buttered 25 cm (10 in) flan tin with the pastry, working your fingers around the side of the tin to make sure the pastry is pushed down into the corners. Trim off any excess pastry using a small knife.

Prick the base of the pastry shell with a fork and rest for 30 minutes. Line the pastry with baking paper, then add baking beans, pastry weights or rice. Bake blind for 15 minutes in the preheated oven. Remove the paper and pastry weights and bake for a further 5 minutes to crisp the pastry.

Leave the oven at 180°C (350°F/Gas 4) and in a bowl, whisk together ricotta, caster sugar, eggs, vanilla, cream and flour with the grated zest and lemon juice. Spoon ricotta mix into cooked pastry shell. Sprinkle with cinnamon and bake in preheated oven for 40 minutes, or until firm.

VARIATIONS

Quince and ricotta tart
Slice 2 cooked quinces. Add to cooked pastry shell, then pour ricotta mix over.

Port-soaked prune and ricotta tart
Soak 300 g (10 ½ oz) pitted prunes in 2 tbsp port for 20 minutes.
Add to cooked pastry shell, then pour ricotta mix over.

Date and orange ricotta tart
Substitute orange for lemon juice and zest. Add 300 g (10 ½ oz)
fresh dates to cooked pastry shell, then pour ricotta mix over.

Other ideas
Add any fruit you like, such as raspberries, pear slices, or roasted nectarine wedges.
You can also swap the ricotta for fresh goat's curd, mascarpone or fromage frais.

LEMON MERINGUE TART

SWEETCRUST PASTRY SHELL
- 300 g (10 ½ oz/2 cups) plain (all-purpose) flour
- 150 g (5 ¼ oz) soft butter, diced
- pinch of salt
- 1 egg
- 55 g (2 oz/¼ cup) caster (superfine) sugar
- plain (all-purpose) flour for dusting

- 4 eggs
- 185 ml (6 ¼ fl oz/ ¾ cup) thickened cream
- 150 g (5 ¼ oz/⅔ cup) caster (superfine) sugar
- 100 ml (3 ½ fl oz/ ⅓ cup) lemon juice
- zest of 2 lemons
- 4 egg whites
- 300 g (10 ½ oz/1 ⅓ cups) caster (superfine) sugar, additional

SERVES 8

✳ To make the pastry dough, place the flour, butter and salt in a bowl and rub together until the mixture resembles fine breadcrumbs. Break the egg into a separate bowl, add caster sugar and mix lightly. Add to the flour mixture and mix until the pastry comes together. Wrap in plastic wrap and chill for 30 minutes.

✳ Preheat oven to 180°C (350°F /Gas 4).

✳ Roll the pastry on a lightly floured board to 3 mm thickness. Line a buttered 25 cm (10 inch) flan tin with the pastry, working your fingers around the side of the tin to make sure the pastry is pushed down into the corners. Trim off any excess pastry using a small knife.

✳ Prick the base of the pastry shell with a fork and rest for 30 minutes. Line the pastry with baking paper, then add baking beans, pastry weights or rice. Bake blind for 15 minutes in the preheated oven. Remove the paper and pastry weights and bake for a further 5 minutes to crisp the pastry.

✳ Leave the oven on at 180°C (350°F/Gas 4). Next, beat the eggs, cream, caster sugar, lemon juice and zest in a bowl. Strain and pour into the still-warm blind-baked pastry shell. Place in the oven and bake for 30 minutes, or until the filling is just set. Set aside to cool.

* While the tart is cooking, make the meringue topping. Beat egg whites until stiff. Add additional caster sugar, a third at a time, and continue beating until meringue is glossy and firm.

* Once the lemon tart has cooled, spoon the meringue over the top of the tart, forming peaks (you may like to use a piping bag to get a more uniform look).

* Place the tart under a very hot preheated grill or in a 220°C (425°F/Gas 7) preheated oven for 3–4 minutes, until just golden brown on top. Allow to cool, then serve.

CHAPTER 3:
BABY CAKES, CUPCAKES AND SCONES

Strawberry
Short Cake

STRAWBERRY SHORTCAKES

- 325 g (11 ½ oz/2 cups plus 1 tbsp) plain (all-purpose) flour
- pinch of salt
- 1 tbsp baking powder
- 55 g (2 oz/¼ cup) caster sugar
- 125 g (4 ½ oz) soft butter, chopped
- 1 egg, beaten
- 125 ml (4 ½ fl oz/½ cup) cream
- 2 tbsp caster (superfine) sugar additional
- 1 egg white, lightly beaten
- 300 g (10 ½ oz) strawberries
- 250 ml (9 fl oz/1 cup) whipped cream

MAKES 8

Preheat oven to 220°C (425°F/Gas 7).

Sift flour, salt and baking powder into a bowl. Add sugar and butter and rub in to produce a fine breadcrumb texture. Whisk egg into cream and pour into flour mixture, bit by bit, stirring it with a fork until mixture holds together.

Turn dough out onto a lightly floured surface and roll to a thickness of 2 cm (⁴/₅ inch). Cut out circles using a 6 cm (2 ½ inch) cutter. Continue re-rolling dough and cutting out circles – you should get 8 in total.

Place shortcakes on a greased baking tray, brush with egg white and sprinkle with remaining caster sugar. Bake for 10–15 minutes, until golden brown.

Split while still warm and fill with sliced strawberries and whipped cream and serve immediately.

LEMON CHEESECAKES WITH BLUEBERRY SAUCE

90 g (3 ¼ oz) gingersnap
biscuits, crushed
40 g (1 ½ oz) unsalted
butter, melted
250 g (9 oz/1 cup) cream
cheese, at room temperature
110 g (3 ¾ oz/½ cup)
caster (superfine) sugar
1 egg
1 ½ tbsp plain (all-purpose) flour
1 tbsp lemon juice
finely grated zest of 1 lemon
150 g (5 ¼ oz/1 cup)
fresh blueberries

BLUEBERRY SAUCE
150 g (5 ¼ oz/1 cup)
fresh blueberries
55 g (2 oz/¼ cup) caster
(superfine) sugar
3 tbsp lemon juice
1 tbsp blueberry jam

MAKES 30

Preheat oven to 150°C (300°F/Gas 2). Line 30 x 30 ml (1 fl oz/⅛ cup) capacity mini-muffin holes with paper cases.

Combine the crushed biscuit and butter in a bowl. Divide between the cases and refrigerate for 15 minutes.

Place the cream cheese and sugar in the bowl of an electric mixer and beat on medium–high speed for 2 minutes. Reduce the speed, add the egg and beat well, scraping down the sides of the bowl as required. Add the flour, lemon juice and zest and combine well.

Transfer the mixture to a large piping bag fitted with a 3 cm (1 ¼ inch) plain nozzle and pipe into the paper cases, filling them three-quarters full. Top each cheesecake with 2–3 blueberries, slightly pushing them into the mixture. Bake for 15 minutes or until set. Cool in the tins for 5 minutes, then turn out onto wire racks and cool for 30 minutes. Refrigerate for at least 3 hours.

＊ Meanwhile, to make the sauce, place all of the ingredients in a saucepan over low heat and stir gently until the sugar has dissolved and the blueberries release some of their juices. Using a slotted spoon, remove the berries and set aside. Increase the heat to high and cook until the liquid has reduced by one-third. Pour over the berries, leave to cool completely, then refrigerate until chilled.

＊ To serve, spoon 1 tablespoon of sauce over each cheesecake.

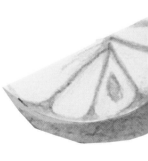

SCONES

- 300 g (10 ½ oz/2 cups) self-raising (self-rising) flour
- pinch of salt
- 2 tsp caster (superfine) sugar
- 125 ml (4 ½ fl oz/½ cup) cream
- 125 ml (4 ½ fl oz/½ cup) milk
- additional cream
- jam and whipped cream for serving

MAKES 6–8

✳ Preheat oven to 200°C (400°F/Gas 6).

✳ Sift together flour, salt and sugar into a bowl. Mix cream and milk together, then stir the wet mix onto the dry mix. Stir gently until the mixture is just combined. Tip mixture onto a lightly floured bench top.

✳ Pat scone dough out with lightly floured hands until it is 2 cm thick. Cut out scones with a 5 ¹/₂ cm (2 ¹/₄ inch) cutter. Mix together leftover bits and roll and cut them out also.

✳ Place scones on a lined baking tray touching together, brush tops with additional cream. Cook in preheated oven for 12–15 minutes.

✳ Remove tray and cover scones with a clean tea towel until cool. Split scones and spread with jam and whipped cream.

ALTERNATIVES

<u>Cinnamon scones</u>
Sift 1 tsp cinnamon with the flour.

<u>Date scones</u>
Add 6–8 finely chopped dates to the scone dough.

BABY PAVLOVAS WITH FRESH BERRIES

6 egg whites
440 g (15 ½ oz/2 cups) caster sugar
1 tsp vanilla extract
1 tbsp cornflour (corn starch)
1 ½ tsp white vinegar
300 ml (10 ¼ fl oz/1 ¼ cups) whipping cream
100 g (4 oz/¾ cup) raspberries
100 g (4 oz/¾ cup) strawberries
100 g (4 oz/¾ cup) blueberries

SERVES 6–8

Preheat oven to 180°C (350°F/Gas 4).

Beat the egg whites until stiff peaks form. Add sugar, one-third at a time, allowing each third to be well incorporated so that you end up with a thick glossy meringue. Fold through the vanilla, cornflour and vinegar.

Spoon tablespoons of meringue on to baking trays lined with baking paper: the mix should make 12–16, depending on the size. Place in the oven, lower the temperature to 120°C (250°F/Gas ½) and bake for 30 minutes. Turn the oven off, leaving the pavlovas to cool inside the oven.

Whip cream to soft peaks. Hull and halve the strawberries. Arrange one pavlova on each plate, spoon cream on top of each. Decorate with a mixture of the berries and serve.

CHOCOLATE BROWNIES

- 180 g (6 ½ oz) butter
- 180 g (6 ½ oz) dark chocolate, chopped
- 3 eggs
- 1 tsp vanilla extract
- 250 g (9 oz/1 cup plus 2 tbsp) caster sugar
- 110 g (3 ¾ oz/$^{2}/^{3}$ cup plus 1 tbsp) plain (all-purpose) flour
- ½ tsp salt
- 180 g (6 ½ oz/1 ½ cups) chopped walnuts

MAKES 12

Preheat oven to 180°C (350°F/Gas 4).

Butter and line a shallow tin.

Melt the butter and chocolate together by placing them in a bowl over a saucepan of simmering water or in a microwave on low for 1–2 minutes. Beat the eggs, vanilla and caster sugar together until light and doubled in bulk. Sift the flour and salt together. Add the flour, melted chocolate and walnuts to the beaten eggs and mix to combine.

Pour into the prepared tin and bake in the preheated oven for 25 minutes. Take care not to overcook the brownies or they will lose their deliciously gooey texture. Allow to cool before cutting.

BABY ORANGE AND ALMOND CAKES

- 2 oranges
- 5 eggs
- 220 g (7 ¾ oz/1 cup) caster (superfine) sugar
- 250 g (9 oz/2 ½ cups) ground almonds
- 1 tsp baking powder

MAKES 18

* Put oranges in a small saucepan, cover with water and bring to the boil.

* Reduce heat to a simmer and cook for 30–40 minutes, or until the fruit is soft. Allow to cool. Cut into quarters, removing pips. Puree in a food processor until smooth.

* Preheat oven to 180°C (350°F/Gas 4).

* Beat eggs and sugar together until pale and doubled in bulk, about 5 minutes. Mix almonds and baking powder together. Add orange puree and almond mixture to the beaten eggs and beat to incorporate completely.

* Line 18 × 125 ml (½ cup) muffin pans with paper cases then spoon the mixture into the prepared muffin pans and bake in the preheated oven for around 20 minutes, or until light brown and firm in the centre. Test the cakes by inserting a skewer into one of them. If it comes out clean, they are ready; if it doesn't, cook for a further 5 minutes and test again. Allow to cool on a wire rack.

CUPCAKES

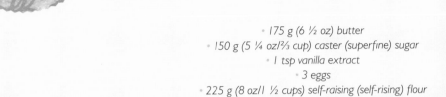

* 175 g (6 ½ oz) butter
* 150 g (5 ¼ oz/⅔ cup) caster (superfine) sugar
* 1 tsp vanilla extract
* 3 eggs
* 225 g (8 oz/1 ½ cups) self-raising (self-rising) flour

BASIC ICING
* 1 ½ tbsp water
* 2 tbsp melted butter
* 130 g (4 ½ oz/1 cup) icing (confectioners') sugar

MAKES 10

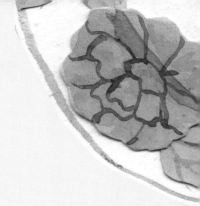

Preheat oven to 180°C (350°F/Gas 5).

Line 10 × 125 ml (½ cup) muffin pans with paper cases.

Cream butter and sugar until light and fluffy. Add vanilla, then eggs one by one, fully incorporating each one before adding the next. Sift flour and fold in carefully. Spoon mixture into the cases. Bake for 15 minutes or until a skewer inserted into the centre comes out clean. Cool completely.

To make the icing, whisk the water and butter together. Add it to the icing sugar, bit by bit, until you reach the desired consistency.

ALTERNATIVES

Coffee icing
Substitute strong coffee for water.

Chocolate icing
Substitute cocoa powder for 30 g (1 oz) of the icing sugar.

Passionfruit icing
Strain 2 passionfruit and use in place of water.

Lemon icing
Substitute lemon juice for water and add the
finely chopped zest of 1 lemon.

Orange icing
Substitute orange juice for water and add the
finely chopped zest of 1 orange.

BANANA DAIQUIRI CUPCAKES

* 150 g (5 ¼ oz/1 cup)
plain (all-purpose) flour
* ½ tsp bicarbonate of
soda (baking soda)
* ¼ tsp baking powder
* 175 g (6 oz/about 2) mashed banana
* 3 tbsp buttermilk
* 30 ml (1 fl oz) dark rum
* 65 g (2 ⅓ oz) unsalted butter,
at room temperature
* 95 g (3 ⅓ oz/½ cup lightly
packed) soft brown sugar
* 1 egg

COCONUT AND RUM FROSTING
* 2 egg whites
* 110 g (3 ¾ oz/½ cup)
caster (superfine) sugar
* 3 tbsp glucose syrup
* 40 ml (1 ¼ fl oz) dark rum
* 1 tsp natural coconut extract
* 30 g (1 oz/½ cup) shredded
coconut, toasted (optional)

MAKES 36

Preheat oven to 180°C (350°F/Gas 4). Line 36 x 30 ml (1 fl oz/⅛ cup) capacity mini-muffin holes with paper cases.

Sift the flour, bicarbonate of soda and baking powder together into a bowl. Combine the banana, buttermilk and rum. Place the butter and sugar in the bowl of an electric mixer and beat on medium speed for 2–3 minutes. Add the egg and beat well. Add the banana mixture, in 3 batches, alternating with the flour mixture, scraping down the sides of the bowl as required.

Transfer the batter to a large piping bag fitted with a 1 cm (½ inch) plain nozzle and pipe into the cases, filling them three-quarters full. Bake for 10 minutes or until lightly golden and they spring back lightly to the touch. Cool in the tins for 1–2 minutes, then turn out onto wire racks to cool completely.

To make the frosting, place the egg white, sugar, glucose and 2 tablespoons water in the top of a double boiler over medium heat and, using electric beaters, beat for 7 minutes or until glossy and stiff. Add the rum and coconut extract and beat for a further minute. Immediately frost the cupcakes and top with the shredded coconut.

LEMON MERINGUE CUPCAKES

- 185 g (6 ½ oz/1 ¼ cups) plain (all-purpose) flour
- 1 ½ tsp baking powder
- 125 g (4 ½ oz) unsalted butter, at room temperature
- 145 g (5 ¼ oz/⅔ cup) caster (superfine) sugar
- 2 eggs
- 125 ml (4 ½ fl oz/½ cup) milk
- ½ tsp natural lemon extract

- 1 tbsp finely grated lemon zest
- 60 g (2 ¼ oz/¼ cup) storebought lemon curd

MERINGUE
- 130 g (4 ¾ oz/½ cup) caster (superfine) sugar
- 95 g (3 ⅓ oz) egg white
- ⅛ tsp salt

MAKES 12

❋ Preheat oven to 175°C (340°F/Gas 3–4). Line 12 x 80 ml (2 ⅓ fl oz/½ cup) capacity muffin holes with paper cases. Sift the flour and baking powder together into a bowl. Place the butter and sugar in the bowl of an electric mixer and beat for 2–3 minutes or until light and creamy. Add the eggs, one at a time, beating well after each addition. Add the flour mixture, in 3 batches, alternating with the milk and beat until combined, scraping down the sides of the bowl as required. Add the lemon extract and zest and beat to combine. Divide between the cases and bake for 18–20 minutes or until lightly golden and when a skewer inserted into the centre comes out clean. Cool in the tin for 4–5 minutes, then turn out onto wire racks to cool completely.

❋ Using a melon baller, remove a scoop of cake from each cupcake. Fill each hole with 1–1 ½ tablespoons of lemon curd.

❋ To make the meringue, place all of the ingredients in the top of a double boiler over medium heat and whisk continuously for 3–4 minutes or until the mixture is hot to the touch and reaches 50°C (122°F) on a candy thermometer. Remove the bowl and, using electric beaters, beat the mixture on high speed until glossy and stiff peaks form. Immediately cover each cupcake with meringue, using a spatula, then lightly toast with a kitchen blowtorch.

KILLER CUPCAKES

- 100 g (3 ½ oz) soft butter
- 130 g (4 ½ oz/⅔ cup) brown sugar
- 1 egg
- 1 tsp vanilla extract
- 95 g (3 ½ oz) dark chocolate, melted and cooled
- 200 g (7 oz/1 ⅓ cups) self-raising (self-rising) flour
- 60 ml (2 fl oz/¼ cup) milk

CHOCOLATE FUDGE ICING
- 220 g (1 cup) caster (super fine) sugar
- 50 g (½ cup) cocoa
- 125 g (4 oz) butter
- 60 ml (¼ cup) milk
- 390 g (3 cups) icing (confectioners') sugar

MAKES 10

Preheat oven to 180°C (350°F/Gas 4).

Line 10 × 125 ml (½ cup) muffin pans with paper cases.

Cream the butter and brown sugar until light and fluffy. Add the egg and vanilla and beat until well incorporated. Stir in the melted chocolate. Fold through flour and milk, and mix until just combined.

Spoon the mixture into the prepared muffin tins and bake in the preheated oven for 15 minutes, or until a skewer inserted into the centre comes out clean. Cool on a wire rack before icing.

To make the Chocolate Fudge Icing, place the caster sugar and cocoa in a saucepan and whisk in the butter and milk. Bring to the boil and cook for 3 minutes, stirring well. Remove from heat and allow to cool until the saucepan is cool enough to touch. Whisk in the icing sugar and stir until thick. Allow to cool completely before spreading onto the cupcakes.

CHAPTER 4:
BISCUITS, BUNS AND SLICES

PASSIONFRUIT
YOYO BISCUITS

- 300 g (10 ½ oz/2 cups) plain (all-purpose) flour
- 300 g (10 ½ oz) soft butter
- 100 g (3 ½ oz/⅔ cup) icing (confectioners') sugar
- 100 g (3 ½ oz/¾ cup) custard powder
- pinch of salt
- ½ tsp vanilla extract
- 2 passionfruit
- 60 g (2 oz) melted butter
- 250 g (9 oz/1 ½ cups) icing (confectioners') sugar, additional

MAKES 18

✳ Preheat oven to 180°C (350°F/Gas 4).

✳ Beat together flour, butter, icing sugar, custard powder, salt and vanilla. Roll into small balls and place on a greased baking tray. Press down with the prongs of a fork to form a round biscuit. Bake in preheated oven for 10–15 minutes, until cooked but not coloured. Allow to cool completely.

✳ Strain the pulp from passionfruit to remove seeds. Mix with butter and icing sugar until smooth. Spoon a small amount of passionfruit butter onto one biscuit half and top with another biscuit. Continue until all biscuits are ready.

CHELSEA BUNS

400 g (14 oz/2 ⅔ cups)
plain (all-purpose) flour
2 sachets (14 g) dried yeast
55 g (2 oz/¼ cup) caster
(superfine) sugar
pinch of salt
100 g (3 ½ oz) melted butter
2 eggs, lightly beaten
125 ml (4 ½ fl oz/½ cup) milk
60 g (2 oz) melted butter, additional

55 g (2 oz/¼ cup) caster
(superfine) sugar, additional
30 g (1 oz/¼ cup) currants
60 g (1 oz/⅓ cup) sultanas

SUGAR SYRUP
125 ml (4 ½ fl oz/½ cup) water
110 g (3 ¾ oz/½ cup)
caster (superfine) sugar

MAKES 12 BUNS

❋ Place the caster sugar and water in a medium-sized saucepan over a low heat. Stir until the sugar dissolves. Raise heat and bring to the boil. Simmer for 2–3 minutes. Allow to cool and use as directed.

❋ Sift flour into a large bowl. Add yeast, sugar and salt and mix briefly. Mix melted butter with beaten eggs and milk. Pour onto flour, mix briefly with a wooden spoon, then tip out onto a floured bench. Knead for 4–5 minutes or until dough is smooth and silky. Place dough in a bowl, cover with plastic wrap and set aside in a warm place to prove until doubled in bulk, about 1–2 hours.

❋ Tip dough onto floured surface and knead well. Roll out to a large square, about 30 cm (12 inches). Brush with additional melted butter, then sprinkle liberally with additional caster sugar. Sprinkle with dried fruits. Roll up from one end to form a large Swiss roll shape. Cut into 2 cm ($^4/_5$ inch) slices. Place slices, cut side up, onto a lined baking tray. Cover tray with a tea towel and prove in a warm place for 20 minutes.

❋ Preheat oven to 200°C (400°F/Gas 6).

❋ Place proved buns in oven and bake for 15–20 minutes, or until risen and golden brown. When buns are cooked brush liberally with Sugar Syrup and allow to cool slightly before eating them warm.

ALTERNATIVES

Swiss buns
Drizzle cooked buns with plain icing.

Jam swirls
Omit butter, sugar and fruit and spread dough with jam instead.

Cheat's hot cross buns
Add 60 g (2 oz) chopped candied orange peel or mixed peel to bun dough. Slash tops with a knife to form cross shapes.

ORANGE AND WALNUT FLORENTINES

· 45 g (1 ½ oz) butter
· 125 ml (4 ½ fl oz/½ cup) pure cream
· 125 g (4 ½ oz/½ cup plus 1 tbsp) caster (superfine) sugar
· 100 g (3 ½ fl oz/¾ cups) walnuts, roughly chopped
· zest of 1 orange, finely chopped
· 50 g (2 oz/⅓ cup) plain (all-purpose) flour
· 100 g (3 ½ oz) dark chocolate, chopped

MAKES 24

Preheat oven to 160°C (325°F/Gas 3).

Place butter, cream and sugar in a small saucepan and bring to the boil over a medium heat, then remove immediately. Stir in the nuts, orange zest and flour. Leave to cool for 5 minutes.

Drop heaped teaspoons of the mix onto lined baking trays, leaving 4 cm (1 ½ inches) between each one.

Bake in preheated oven for 15–20 minutes. Biscuits should be golden at the edges and firm to the touch. Allow to cool on the trays.

Melt chocolate and spread onto the back of each biscuit. Allow chocolate to set completely before storing.

VIENNESE BISCUITS

• 250 g (9 oz) soft butter
• 130 g (4 ½ oz/1 cup) icing (confectioners') sugar
• 2 eggs
• 250 g (9 oz/1 ⅔ cup) plain (all-purpose) flour

MAKES 40

✳ Preheat oven to 200°C (400°F/Gas 6).

✳ Cream butter and sugar until white and fluffy. Add eggs, beat well, then beat in flour. Place mixture into a piping bag and pipe onto buttered baking trays or trays lined with baking paper.

✳ Bake in preheated oven for 8–10 minutes, or until beginning to brown at the edges.

GINGERBREAD HEARTS

- 125 g (4 ½ oz) soft butter
- 70 g (2 ½ oz/⅓ cup) brown sugar
- zest of 1 orange, finely chopped
- 1 egg
- 125 ml (4 ½ fl oz/½ cup) warm honey
- 450 g (16 oz/3 cups) self-raising (self-rising) flour
- 4 tsp ground ginger
- ½ tsp ground cinnamon
- 30 blanched almonds
- 1 egg, lightly beaten
- raw sugar

MAKES 30 BISCUITS

Preheat oven to 170°C (325°F/Gas 3).

Cream butter and sugar until light and fluffy. Add zest and egg and beat until smooth. Stir in honey. Sift together flour, ginger and cinnamon and stir into wet mixture. Wrap biscuit mixture in plastic wrap and chill for 30 minutes.

Roll biscuit mixture out onto a floured surface and cut out heart shapes. Lay biscuits on a lined baking tray. Push an almond into the centre of each. Brush each biscuit with beaten egg and sprinkle raw sugar over. Bake in preheated oven for 8–10 minutes.

Allow biscuits to cool before serving.

RASPBERRY
COCONUT SLICE

• 125 g (4 ½ oz) soft butter
• 55 g (2 oz/¼ cup) caster (superfine) sugar
• ½ tsp vanilla extract
• I egg
• 225 g (8 oz/I ½ cups) self-raising (self-rising) flour
• 60 ml (2 fl oz/¼ cup) milk
• 160 g (5 ¾ oz/½ cup) raspberry jam
• 150 g (5 ¼ oz/I ¼ cups) raspberries
• 100 g (3 ½ oz) soft butter, additional
• 110 g (3 ¾ oz/½ cup) caster (superfine) sugar, additional
• 2 eggs, additional
• 225 g (8 oz/2 ½ cups) shredded coconut
• 50 g (2 oz/⅓ cup) plain (all-purpose) flour, additional
• icing (confectioners) sugar to serve

MAKES 12 GENEROUS SLICES; 48 BITE-SIZED

Preheat oven to 180°C (350°F/Gas 4).

Butter a shallow tin, line the sides and bottom with baking paper and butter lightly.

Cream the butter, caster sugar and vanilla in a mixer until white and fluffy. Add the egg, then fold in flour and milk. Mix until it forms a sticky dough. Press the dough into the prepared tin. Spread jam over the uncooked base, then sprinkle evenly with raspberries.

Cream the additional butter and caster sugar together until pale and fluffy. Add the eggs, one at a time and beating well after each addition. Stir in the coconut and flour, then gently spoon the mix over the raspberry base.

Bake in the preheated oven for 35–40 minutes. Check that the topping is cooked in the centre. If not, cook for another 5–10 minutes. Allow to cool before cutting into slices. Dust with icing sugar to serve.

MILLIONAIRE'S SHORTBREAD (CARAMEL SLICE)

* 90 g (3 ¼ oz) soft butter
* 90 g (3 ¼ oz/⅓ cup) raw sugar
* 1 egg
* 60 g (2 oz/⅓ cup) self-raising (self-rising) flour
* 60 g (2 oz/¾ cup) desiccated coconut
* 395 ml (13 ½ fl oz) can condensed milk
* 125 g (4 ½ oz) butter, additional
* 125 g (4 ½ oz/½ cup) caster (superfine) sugar, additional
* 150 g (5 ¼ oz) dark chocolate, chopped

MAKES 12 GENEROUS SLICES; 48 BITE-SIZED

❋ Preheat oven to 180°C (350°F/Gas 4).

❋ Cream butter and sugar until light and fluffy. Add egg, beat well. Add flour and coconut and stir to combine. Spread mixture in lined shallow tin. Bake in heated oven for 15–20 minutes, or until just cooked. (It's going to go back into the oven for another 15 minutes, so it doesn't have to be brown.)

❋ Place condensed milk, butter and additional sugar in a small saucepan. Place over a medium heat and bring to the boil, stirring often to prevent condensed milk catching and burning. When sugar is dissolved and mixture has just started to boil, pour it over the cooked pastry base. Return to oven and cook for a further 10–15 minutes, or until caramel has turned golden brown. Set aside to cool.

❋ When caramel is set, melt chocolate and coat caramel. Top evenly, leave to set, then cut into squares.

CHAPTER 5:
PETITE PASTRIES

STRAWBERRY TARTLETS WITH STICKY BALSAMIC GLAZE

300 g (10 ½ oz/1 ¼ cup) goat's curd
200 g (7 oz/⅔ cup) ricotta
3 tsp orange blossom honey
1 tsp finely grated orange zest
25 strawberries, halved

VANILLA SHORTCRUST PASTRY
125 g (4 ½ oz) unsalted
butter, at room temperature
80 g (2 ¾ oz/⅔ cup) icing
(confectioners') sugar
1 egg yolk
½ vanilla bean, split
and seeds scraped
200 g (7 oz/1 ⅓ cup) plain
(all-purpose) flour, sifted

BALSAMIC GLAZE
125 ml (4 ½ fl oz/½ cup) good
quality balsamic vinegar
115 g (4 oz/⅓ cup) honey

MAKES ABOUT 50

* To make the pastry, place the butter and icing sugar in the bowl of an electric mixer and beat for 2–3 minutes or until light and creamy. Add the egg yolk and vanilla seeds and beat to combine well. Add the flour and beat until just combined. Turn the dough out onto a floured surface, shape into a disc, wrap in plastic wrap and refrigerate for 1–2 hours.

* Preheat oven to 180°C (350°F/Gas 4).

* Meanwhile, to make the glaze, place the vinegar and honey in a saucepan over medium heat and simmer until reduced by one-third and the mixture is thick and syrupy. Cool completely.

* Roll the dough into 50 x 8 g (¼ oz) balls. Place each ball in a 3 ½ cm (1 ¼ inch) fluted tartlet tin and press the pastry into the base and sides. Freeze for 10 minutes.

Place the pastry cases on baking trays and bake for 7–9 minutes or until golden and cooked. If the pastry puffs up, use a teaspoon to gently push it down. Cool in the tins for 8–10 minutes, then turn out onto wire racks and cool completely.

To serve, combine the goat's curd, ricotta, honey and orange zest in a bowl. Transfer to a large piping bag fitted with a 5 mm (^{1}/$_4$ inch) plain nozzle and pipe the mixture into the cases. Top each with a strawberry half and drizzle with the balsamic glaze.

PROFITEROLES WITH WHITE CHOCOLATE AND RASPBERRIES

300 g (10 ½ oz/2 cups) raspberries

CHOUX PASTRY
125 ml (4 ½ fl oz/½ cup) water
125 ml (4 ½ fl oz/½ cup) milk
pinch of salt
100 g (3 ½ oz) butter
150 g (5 ¼ oz/1 cup)
plain (all-purpose) flour
5 eggs

FILLING
2 egg yolks
55 g (2 oz/¼ cup) caster
(superfine) sugar
1 tbsp plain (all-purpose) flour
500 ml (17 fl oz/2 cups) milk
½ tsp vanilla extract
100 g (3 ½ oz) white
chocolate, chopped

WHITE CHOCOLATE SAUCE
90 g (3 ¼ oz) white
chocolate, chopped
1 tbsp butter
2 tbsp brandy
80 ml (2 ¾ fl oz/⅓ cup) cream

MAKES 30

✳ To make the pastry, place the water, milk, salt and butter in a saucepan and bring to the boil. Tip in the flour, stir and return to a low heat. Cook for 2–3 minutes, stirring constantly, until the mixture begins to come away from the side of the saucepan.

✳ Tip the contents into a food processor. Start the processor, allowing the mixture to cool slightly. Break the eggs into a jug and beat lightly. Slowly add the egg mix to the pastry mixture, ensuring that the eggs are well incorporated each time before adding more. Continue adding the eggs until the pastry is of a dropping consistency – not too runny. You may not need to add all the eggs; it tends to vary a bit from batch to batch.

✳ Preheat oven to 200°C (400°F/Gas 6).

✳ Spoon teaspoonfuls of choux pastry onto lined baking trays. Place the trays in the oven at the same time. It is important not to open the door during the first 10 minutes of cooking, as cold draughts will make the pastry sink.

✳ Cook for 10 minutes, then reduce oven temperature to 180°C (350°F/Gas 4). Cook for another 10 minutes, then try one. They should be quite brown (more than golden brown) and relatively dry inside. Resist the urge to take them out too soon, because you will not fit enough cream into them if they are doughy inside. When ready, set aside to cool.

✳ Beat the egg yolks and caster sugar together until pale, then stir in flour until smooth. Bring the milk and vanilla to the boil. Whisk the hot milk into the egg yolk mixture and return to a clean saucepan over a low heat. Stir constantly as the custard comes to the boil and thickens. Remove from heat. Add chopped chocolate and stir until it dissolves.

✳ When cold, spoon the custard into a piping bag, if you have one, then poke the piping nozzle into the choux pastry base and squeeze to fill each one. If not using a piping bag, slit the profiteroles with a knife and fill with custard. Refrigerate until ready to serve.

✳ Make the sauce by placing all the ingredients in a heatproof bowl. Set the bowl over a saucepan of simmering water and cook for 5–6 minutes. Stir often until everything has melted together smoothly.

✳ To serve, either arrange 3–4 profiteroles on each plate (piled if you wish) or the entire batch on a large platter. Warm the chocolate sauce, then drizzle it over the profiteroles. Scatter raspberries over and serve.

WARM APPLE PIE BITES

* 20 g (¾ oz) unsalted butter
* 400 g (14 oz/about 3) granny smith apples, peeled, cored and diced
* 45 g (1 ½ oz/¼ cup) lightly packed) soft brown sugar
* ½ tsp ground cinnamon, plus 2 tsp ground cinnamon extra, for coating
* ½ tsp ground nutmeg
* 2 tbsp orange juice
* 2 tsp cornflour
* 2 tsp finely grated orange zest
* 220 g (7 ¾ oz/1 cup) caster (superfine) sugar
* vegetable oil, for deep-frying

DOUGH
* 375 g (13 oz/2 ½ cups) plain (all-purpose) flour
* 2 tsp caster (superfine) sugar
* 150 g (5 ½ oz) cold unsalted butter, cut into 12 pieces
* 125 ml (4 ½ fl oz/½ cup) buttermilk

MAKES 15–16

To make the dough, place the flour, sugar and butter in the bowl of a food processor and pulse until the mixture resembles breadcrumbs. Add the buttermilk and pulse until the dough comes together to form a ball. Turn out onto a floured surface, shape into a disc, wrap in plastic wrap and refrigerate for 2 hours.

Meanwhile, place the butter, apple, brown sugar, cinnamon and nutmeg in a frying pan over medium heat and cook for 5–6 minutes or until the apple has softened. Combine the orange juice and cornflour to make a paste, add to the apple mixture and cook for 1 minute or until thickened. Add the orange zest and cool to room temperature.

Roll out the dough on a floured surface to 3 mm (⅛ inch) and, using a 9 cm (3 ½ inch) round cutter, cut out circles. Re-roll the scraps and repeat. Place 2 teaspoons of apple mixture in the centre of each circle, fold in half and pinch the edges together firmly to seal. Refrigerate for 15–20 minutes.

* Combine the caster sugar and extra cinnamon together in a shallow bowl and set aside.

* Heat the oil in a deep-fryer or large, heavy-based frying pan to 175°C (340°F). Deep-fry the pies, 3–4 at a time, for 1–2 minutes on each side or until lightly golden. Drain on kitchen paper, then roll in the cinnamon sugar to coat. Serve immediately.

CHOCOLATE ÉCLAIRS

ÉCLAIRS
- *125 ml (4 ½ fl oz/½ cup) water*
- *125 ml (4 ½ fl oz/½ cup) milk*
- *pinch of salt*
- *100 g (3 ½ oz) butter*
- *150 g (5 ¼ oz/1 cup) plain (all-purpose) flour*
- *5 eggs*

CUSTARD
- *2 egg yolks*
- *55 g (2 oz/¼ cup) caster (superfine) sugar*
- *1 tbsp plain (all-purpose) flour*
- *500 ml (17 fl oz/2 cups) milk*
- *½ tsp vanilla extract*

CHOCOLATE GANACHE
- *2 tbsp cream*
- *90 g (3 ¼ oz) dark chocolate, chopped*

MAKES 12–15

Preheat oven to 200°C (400°F/Gas 6).

To make the pastry, place the water, milk, salt and butter in a saucepan and bring to the boil. Tip in the flour, stir and return to a low heat. Cook for 2–3 minutes, stirring constantly, until the mixture begins to come away from the side of the saucepan.

Tip the contents into a food processor. Start the processor, allowing the mixture to cool slightly. Break the eggs into a jug and beat lightly. Slowly add the egg mix to the pastry mixture, ensuring that the eggs are well incorporated each time before adding more. Continue adding the eggs until the pastry is of a dropping consistency – not too runny. You may not need to add all the eggs; it tends to vary a bit from batch to batch.

Pipe 8 cm (3 inch) lengths of choux pastry onto lined baking trays. Place the trays in the oven at the same time. It is important not to open the door during the first 10 minutes of cooking, as cold draughts will make the pastry sink.

Cook for 10 minutes, then reduce oven temperature to 180°C (350°F/Gas 4). Cook for another 10 minutes, then try one. They should be quite brown (more than golden brown) and relatively dry inside. Resist the urge to take them out too soon, as they will end up doughy inside. When ready, set aside to cool.

In the meantime, make the custard. Beat the egg yolks and caster sugar together until pale, then stir in the flour until smooth.

Place the milk and vanilla in a saucepan and bring to the boil. Whisk the hot milk into the egg-yolk mixture, then pour into a clean saucepan.

Place the custard over a low heat and stir constantly as the custard comes to the boil and thickens. Remove from heat. This custard can be made in advance and reheated gently over a low heat when needed. Cover with plastic wrap if not using immediately to stop a skin forming.

Spoon the thick custard into a piping bag, if you have one, then poke the piping nozzle into the choux pastry base and squeeze to fill with pastry cream. If not using a piping bag, slit the eclairs with a knife and fill with custard.

Make the ganache by warming the cream to just below boiling, then removing it from heat. Add chocolate and whisk to incorporate. Spread ganache over the top of each eclair.

earl grey

english
breakfast

oolong

PECAN CARAMEL
TARTLETS

- 60 g (2 ¼ oz) unsalted butter
- 90 g (3 ¼ oz/¼ cup) dark corn syrup (see note)
- 1 tbsp honey
- 65 g (2 ⅓ oz/½ cup) icing (confectioners') sugar
- 50 g (1 ¾ oz/½ cup) pecans, finely chopped
- ½ teaspoon natural vanilla extract

CREAM CHEESE PASTRY
- 125 g (4 ½ oz) butter, at room temperature
- 90 g (3 ¼ oz/⅓ cup) cream cheese, at room temperature
- 150 g (5 ½ oz/1 cup) plain (all-purpose) flour
- 30 g (1 oz/¼ cup) icing (confectioners') sugar
- ¼ tsp salt

MAKES 24

※ Preheat oven to 180°C (350°F/Gas 4). Grease 24 x 30 ml (1 fl oz/⅛ cup) capacity mini-muffin holes.

※ To make the pastry, place the butter and cream cheese in the bowl of an electric mixer and beat on medium speed for 1–2 minutes or until combined. Add the flour, icing sugar and salt and beat to combine. Divide the pastry into 24 balls and place one in each muffin hole. Cover and refrigerate for 15–20 minutes.

※ Press the pastry into the base and sides of each hole. Cover and refrigerate until required. Place the butter, corn syrup, honey and icing sugar in a saucepan over medium heat, bring to the boil and cook for 1 minute. Remove from the heat, add the pecans and vanilla extract and stir to combine.

※ Spoon into the pastry cases and bake for 20–25 minutes or until set. Cool in the tins for 10 minutes, then remove and cool completely on wire racks.

NOTE: Dark corn syrup is available from specialty grocery shops.

CHOCOLATE TARTS
WITH RASPBERRY

- 400 g (14 oz) dark chocolate (65% cocoa solids), finely chopped
- 550 ml (19 fl oz/ 2 ¼ cups) thickened cream
- 2 tbsp natural raspberry extract (optional)
- 50 fresh raspberries

CHOCOLATE SHORTCRUST PASTRY
- 175 g (6 oz/1 ¼ cups) plain (all-purpose) flour
- 25 g (1 oz/¼ cup) cocoa powder
- 125 g (4 ½ oz) unsalted butter, at room temperature
- 80 g (2 ¾ oz/⅔ cup) icing (confectioners') sugar
- 1 egg yolk

MAKES ABOUT 50

✳ Place the chocolate and cream in the top of a double boiler over medium heat and stir until melted and smooth. Mix in the raspberry extract, if using. Transfer to a bowl and refrigerate for 20 minutes. Remove and stir, then refrigerate for a further 20 minutes. Repeat the process twice more and continue chilling for 4 hours or overnight.

✳ Meanwhile, to make the pastry, sift the flour and cocoa together into a bowl. Place the butter and icing sugar in the bowl of an electric mixer and beat for 1–2 minutes or until light and creamy. Add the egg yolk and combine well. Add the flour mixture and beat until just combined. Shape into a disc, wrap in plastic wrap and refrigerate for 1–2 hours.

✳ Preheat the oven to 180°C (350°F/Gas 4).

✳ Roll the dough into 50 x 8 g (¼ oz) balls. Place each ball in a 3 ½ cm (1 ¼ inch) fluted tartlet tin and press the pastry into the base and sides. Freeze for 10 minutes.

✳ Place the pastry cases on baking trays and bake for 7–9 minutes or until golden and cooked. If the pastry puffs up, use a teaspoon to gently push it down. Cool in the tins for 8–10 minutes, then turn out onto wire racks to cool completely.

✳ Transfer the chocolate mixture to the bowl of an electric mixer and beat on medium speed for 1–2 minutes or until soft peaks form. Transfer to a large piping bag fitted with a 5 mm (¼ inch) plain nozzle and pipe into the cases. Top with a raspberry.

CHAPTER 6:
CAKE POPS, WHOOPIE PIES AND MACAROONS

RASPBERRY MACAROONS WITH WHITE CHOCOLATE

120 g (4 ¼ oz/1 ¼ cups) almond meal (ground almonds)
220 g (7 ¾ oz/2 cups) icing (confectioners') sugar
110 g (3 ¾ oz) egg white
30 g (1 oz/½ cup) caster (superfine) sugar
2 tsp natural raspberry extract
pink food colouring, paste or powdered is preferable

WHITE CHOCOLATE GANACHE
120 g (4 ¼ oz) white chocolate, chopped
2 ½ tbsp pouring (single) cream
2 tsp natural raspberry extract
3 tsp raspberry jam

MAKES ABOUT 30

Line 2 baking trays with baking paper. Process the almond meal and icing sugar in a food processor until combined, then sift twice. Place the egg white in the bowl of an electric mixer and beat on medium speed until frothy, then increase the speed while gradually adding the caster sugar. Continue beating until stiff peaks form, then mix in the raspberry extract and enough colouring for desired effect. Fold one third into the almond mixture and combine well. Gently fold through the remaining egg white mixture; it should be glossy and thick, not thin and runny.

Transfer to a piping bag fitted with a 5 mm (¼ inch) plain nozzle and pipe 3 cm (1 ¼ inch) circles about 3 cm (1 ¼ inches) apart onto the trays. Leave at room temperature for 1–6 hours (depending on the humidity) or until a crust forms; the macaroons should no longer be sticky to the touch.

Preheat oven to 140°C (275°F/Gas 1). Bake the macaroons for 15–18 minutes until they rise slightly. Immediately slide the macaroons and paper off the trays and onto wire racks to cool completely.

Meanwhile, to make the ganache, place the chocolate and cream in the top of a double boiler over medium heat and stir until melted and smooth. Refrigerate for 25–35 minutes or until firm but pliable. Add the raspberry extract and jam and mix well.

Transfer to a small piping bag fitted with a 1 cm (½ inch) plain nozzle and pipe about 1 teaspoon onto half of the macaroons. Sandwich with the remaining macaroons.

GINGER WHOOPIE PIES WITH SPICED CANDIED GINGER CREAM

260 g (9 ¼ oz/1 ¾ cups)
plain (all-purpose) flour
1 tsp bicarbonate of
soda (baking soda)
pinch of salt
1 tsp ground ginger
110 g (3 ¾ oz/½ cup)
caster (superfine) sugar
95 g (3 ⅓ oz/½ cup lightly
packed) brown sugar
125 g (4 ½ oz) unsalted
butter, at room temperature
½ tsp natural vanilla extract
1 egg
250 ml (9 fl oz/1 cup) milk

SPICED CANDIED GINGER CREAM
375 g (13 oz/1 ½ cups) cream
cheese, at room temperature
75 g (2 ¾ oz) unsalted butter,
at room temperature
2 tsp maple syrup
125 g (4 ½ oz/1 cup) icing
(confectioners') sugar
1 tsp ground cinnamon
1 tsp ground nutmeg
35 g (1 ¼ oz) candied
ginger, chopped

MAKES 15

Preheat oven to 175°C (340°F/Gas 3–4). Grease and flour 2 baking trays or 3 whoopie pie tins. Sift the flour, bicarbonate of soda, salt and ginger together into a large bowl. Place the sugars and butter in the bowl of an electric mixer and beat on medium speed for 1–2 minutes or until light and creamy. Add the vanilla extract and egg and beat for a further minute. Reduce the speed and add the flour mixture, in 3 batches, alternating with the milk and beat until combined, scraping down the sides of the bowl as required.

Place 1 ½-tablespoon amounts of batter about 5 cm (2 inches) apart on the trays and bake for 8–10 minutes or until cooked through. Cool for 5 minutes on the trays, then transfer to wire racks to cool completely.

Meanwhile, to make the ginger cream, place the cream cheese and butter in the bowl of an electric mixer and beat on medium speed for 2–3 minutes or until combined and smooth. Reduce the speed and add the maple syrup, icing sugar and spices and beat until combined. Fold in the candied ginger, cover with plastic wrap and refrigerate for 20 minutes or until firm.

Transfer to a piping bag fitted with a 1 cm (½ inch) plain nozzle and pipe 2 tablespoons of filling onto half of the cookies. Sandwich with the remaining cookies.

WALNUT BROWNIE POPS

- 40 lollipop sticks
- 500 g (1 lb 2 oz) dark chocolate (70% cocoa solids), melted
- chocolate sprinkles, for coating

WALNUT BROWNIE
- 300 g (10 ½ oz) dark chocolate (70% cocoa solids), finely chopped
- 185 g (6 ½ oz) unsalted butter, at room temperature
- 330 g (11 ¾ oz/1 ½ cups)

caster (superfine) sugar
- 45 g (1 ¾ oz/¼ cup lightly packed) soft brown sugar
- 4 eggs, lightly beaten
- 2 tsp natural vanilla extract
- 150 g (5 ¼ oz/1 cup) plain (all-purpose) flour
- 2 tbsp cocoa powder
- 100 g (3 ½ oz/1 cup) walnuts, finely chopped

MAKES ABOUT 40

✳ To make the brownie, preheat oven to 175°C (340°F/Gas 3–4). Grease and line a 31 cm x 21 cm x 5 cm (12 ½ inch x 8 ¼ inch x 2 inch) cake tin with baking paper. Place the chocolate and butter in the top of a double boiler over medium heat and stir until melted and smooth. Add the sugars and stir until dissolved. Remove from the heat and cool slightly. Add the egg and vanilla extract and stir to combine. Sift the flour and cocoa together into a large bowl, add the chocolate mixture, combine well and stir in the walnuts.

✳ Pour into the tin and bake for 25–30 minutes or until still fudgy and a skewer inserted into the centre comes out with moist crumbs. Cool completely in the tin.

✳ Line 2 baking trays with baking paper. Using a small ice-cream scoop, scoop out balls of brownie onto the trays. Quickly roll each in the palms of your hands to shape into a neat ball. Insert a stick into each ball and refrigerate for 2 hours or until well chilled and firm.

✳ Carefully dip each brownie pop in the melted chocolate and tap the stick on the side of the bowl while slowly spinning to remove excess chocolate. Roll each pop in the sprinkles to coat well. Stand in Styrofoam to dry. Serve immediately or store in an airtight container in the refrigerator for 3–4 days.

CHOC-MINT WHOOPIE PIES WITH MARSHMALLOW FROSTING

- 150 g (5 ¼ oz/1 cup) plain (all-purpose) flour
- 60 g (2 ¼ oz/½ cup) cocoa powder
- ½ tsp bicarbonate of soda (baking soda)
- 145 g (5 ¼ oz/⅔ cup) caster (superfine) sugar
- 90 g (3 ¼ oz) unsalted butter, at room temperature
- ½ tsp natural vanilla extract
- 1 tsp mint extract

- 1 egg
- 250 ml (9 fl oz/1 cup) milk
- 120 g (4 ¼ oz) crushed peppermint candies, for decoration

MARSHMALLOW FROSTING
- 3 egg whites
- 165 g (5 ¾ oz/¾ cup) caster (superfine) sugar
- ¼ tsp cream of tartar
- 2 tsp peppermint schnapps

MAKES 12

❋ Preheat oven to 175°C (340°F/Gas 3–4). Grease and flour 2 baking trays or 3 whoopie pie tins. Sift the flour, cocoa and bicarbonate of soda together into a large bowl. Place the sugar and butter in the bowl of an electric mixer and beat on medium speed for 1–2 minutes or until light and creamy. Add the vanilla and mint extracts and egg and beat for a further minute. Reduce the speed and add the flour mixture, in 3 batches, alternating with the milk and beat until combined, scraping down the sides of the bowl as required.

❋ Place 1 ½-tablespoon amounts of batter about 5 cm (2 inches) apart on the trays and bake for 8–10 minutes or until cooked through. Cool for 5 minutes on the trays, then transfer to wire racks to cool completely.

❋ Meanwhile, to make the frosting, place the egg white, sugar and cream of tartar in the top of a double boiler over medium heat and whisk for 3 minutes or until warm and the sugar has dissolved. Remove from the heat, add the schnapps and, using electric beaters, beat for 6–7 minutes or until glossy and stiff peaks form.

❋ Transfer to a piping bag fitted with a 1 cm (½ inch) plain nozzle and pipe 2 tablespoons of filling onto half of the cookies. Sandwich with the remaining cookies and roll the sides of the pies in the crushed peppermint candies to coat.

CHOCOLATE MACAROONS
WITH ESPRESSO AND
COCOA NIBS

- 110 g (3 ¾ oz/1 cup) almond meal (ground almonds)
- 15 g (½ oz) cocoa powder
- 200 g (7 oz/1 ½ cups) icing (confectioners') sugar
- 110 g (3 ¾ oz) egg white
- 30 g (1 oz/⅛ cup) caster (superfine) sugar

ESPRESSO GANACHE
- 80 ml (2 ½ fl oz/⅓ cup) pouring (single) cream
- 2 tsp instant coffee granules
- 120 g (4 ¼ oz) dark chocolate (70% cocoa solids), chopped
- 2 tbsp cocoa nibs (see note)

MAKES ABOUT 30

Line 2 baking trays with baking paper. Process the almond meal, cocoa and icing sugar in a food processor until combined, then sift twice. Place the egg white in the bowl of an electric mixer and beat on medium speed until frothy, then increase the speed while gradually adding the caster sugar. Continue beating until stiff peaks form. Fold one-third into the almond mixture and combine well. Gently fold through the remaining egg white mixture; it should be glossy and thick, not thin and runny.

Transfer to a piping bag fitted with a 5 mm (¼ inch) plain nozzle and pipe 3 cm (1 ¼ inch) circles about 3 cm (1 ¼ inches) apart onto the trays. Leave at room temperature for 1–6 hours (depending on the humidity) or until a crust forms; the macaroons should no longer be sticky to the touch.

Preheat oven to 140°C (275°F/Gas 1). Bake the macaroons for 15–18 minutes until they rise slightly. Immediately slide the macaroons and paper off the trays onto wire racks to cool completely.

Meanwhile, to make the ganache, place the cream and coffee granules in the top of a double boiler over medium heat and stir until the coffee has dissolved. Add the chocolate and stir until melted and smooth. Refrigerate for 20–25 minutes or until firm but pliable, then gently stir through the cocoa nibs. Transfer to a small piping bag fitted with a 1 cm (½ inch) plain nozzle and pipe about 1 teaspoon onto half of the macaroons. Sandwich with the remaining macaroons.

 NOTE: Cocoa nibs are available from gourmet food shops.

BLACK VELVET
WHOOPIE PIES

• 225 g (8 oz/1 ½ cups)
plain (all-purpose) flour
• 60 g (2 ¼ oz/½ cup) cocoa powder
• 1 tsp bicarbonate of
soda (baking soda)
• pinch of salt
• 160 g (5 ⅔ oz/1 cup) brown sugar
• 125 g (4 ½ oz) unsalted
butter, at room temperature
• 1 tsp natural vanilla extract
• 1 egg

• 250 ml (9 fl oz/1 cup) buttermilk
• ½ teaspoon white vinegar

CREAM CHEESE FROSTING
• 375 g (13 oz/1 ½ cups) cream
cheese, at room temperature
• 75 g (2 ¾ oz) unsalted butter,
at room temperature
• 1 tsp natural vanilla extract
• 125 g (4 ½ oz/1 cup) icing
(confectioners') sugar, sifted

MAKES 15

Preheat oven to 175°C (340°F/Gas 3–4). Grease and flour 2 baking trays or 3 whoopie pie tins. Sift the flour, cocoa, bicarbonate of soda and salt together into a large bowl. Place the sugar and butter in the bowl of an electric mixer and beat on medium speed for 1–2 minutes or until light and creamy. Add the vanilla extract and egg and beat for a further minute. Reduce the speed and add the flour mixture, in 3 batches, alternating with the buttermilk and beat until just combined, then beat in the vinegar, scraping down the sides of the bowl as required.

Place 1 ½-tablespoon amounts of batter about 5 cm (2 inches) apart on the trays and bake for 8–10 minutes or until cooked through. Cool for 5 minutes on the trays, then transfer to wire racks to cool completely.

Meanwhile, to make the frosting, place the cream cheese, butter and vanilla extract in the bowl of an electric mixer and beat on medium–high speed for 2–3 minutes or until combined and smooth. Reduce the speed, add the icing sugar and beat until combined. Cover with plastic wrap and refrigerate for 20–25 minutes or until firm.

Transfer to a piping bag fitted with a 1 cm (½ inch) plain nozzle and pipe 2 tablespoons of filling onto half of the cookies. Sandwich with the remaining cookies.

GLITTER POPS

- 80 g (2 ¾ oz) unsalted butter, at room temperature
- 250 g (9 oz/1 cup) cream cheese, at room temperature
- 125 g (4 ½ oz/1 cup) icing (confectioners') sugar
- 2 tbsp white chocolate liqueur
- 50 lollipop sticks
- 650 g (1 lb 7 oz) white chocolate, melted
- 5 g (2 ¾ oz/⅓ cup) gold sanding sugar (see note)

WHITE CHOCOLATE CAKE
- 300 g (10 ½ oz/2 cups) plain (all-purpose) flour
- 2 tsp baking powder
- ¼ tsp salt
- 225 g (8 oz) unsalted butter, at room temperature
- 440 g (15 ½ oz/2 cups) caster (superfine) sugar
- 4 eggs
- 85 g (3 oz/⅓ cup) sour cream
- 65 ml (2 ¼ fl oz) white chocolate liqueur
- 65 ml (2 ¼ fl oz) milk
- 1 tbsp white vinegar

MAKES 45–50

✳ To make the cake, preheat oven to 180°C (350°F/Gas 4). Grease and line a 31 cm x 21 cm x 5 cm (12 ½ inch x 8 ¼ inch x 2 inch) cake tin with baking paper. Sift the flour, baking powder and salt together into a bowl. Place the butter and sugar in the bowl of an electric mixer and beat on medium speed for 2–3 minutes or until light and creamy. Add the eggs, one at a time, beating well after each addition. Add the sour cream and liqueur and mix well. Add the milk and vinegar, in 2 batches, alternating with the flour mixture, scraping down the sides of the bowl as required. Pour into the tin and bake for 35–40 minutes or until a skewer inserted into the centre comes out clean. Cool completely in the tin. Slice off the sides, top and bottom of the cake and discard. Finely crumble the remaining cake into a large bowl.

✳ Place the butter and cream cheese in the bowl of an electric mixer and beat on medium speed for 2 minutes or until smooth. Add the icing sugar and liqueur and mix well. Add to the cake crumbs and mix well; the mixture should stick together when squeezed in your hands.

✳ Line 2 baking trays with baking paper and roll the mixture into 30 g (1 oz) balls. Insert a stick into each ball, place on the trays and refrigerate for 30 minutes or until chilled and firm.

✳ Carefully dip each pop in the melted chocolate, gently twirling off any excess. Sprinkle with the sanding sugar and stand in Styrofoam to dry. Serve immediately or store in an airtight container in the refrigerator for 3–4 days.

 <u>N</u>OTE: Sanding sugar is available from specialist cake decorating shops or online.

BLOOD ORANGE
MACAROONS

- 120 g (4 ¼ oz/1 ¼ cups) almond meal (ground almonds)
- 220 g (7 ¾ oz/1 ¾ cups) icing (confectioners') sugar
- 110 g (3 ¾ oz) egg white
- 30 g (1 oz/⅛ cup) caster (superfine) sugar
- 1 tsp natural orange extract
- orange or red food colouring, paste or powdered is preferable

BLOOD ORANGE CURD
- 6 egg yolks
- 125 ml (4 ½ fl oz/½ cup) blood orange juice, strained
- 1 ½ tbsp lemon juice
- 165 g (5 ¾ oz/¾ cup) caster (superfine) sugar
- 80 g (2 ¾ oz) unsalted butter, cubed

MAKES ABOUT 30

Line 2 baking trays with baking paper. Process the almond meal and icing sugar in a food processor until combined, then sift twice. Place the egg white in the bowl of an electric mixer and beat on medium speed until frothy, then increase the speed while gradually adding the caster sugar. Continue beating until stiff peaks form. Mix in the orange extract and colouring. Fold one-third into the almond mixture and combine well. Gently fold through the remaining egg white mixture; it should be glossy and thick, not thin and runny.

Transfer to a piping bag fitted with a 5 mm (¼ inch) plain nozzle and pipe 3 cm (1 ¼ inch) circles about 3 cm (1 ¼ inches) apart onto the trays. Leave for 1–6 hours (depending on the humidity) or until a crust forms; the macaroons should no longer be sticky.

To make the curd, place the egg yolks, juices and sugar in a saucepan over medium–low heat and stir continuously for 8–9 minutes or until thick and the mixture coats a wooden spoon. Remove from the heat and add the butter, 1 cube at a time, beating well after each addition. Cover with plastic wrap and refrigerate for 1 hour.

Preheat the oven to 140°C (275°F/Gas 1). Bake the macaroons for 15–18 minutes until they rise slightly. Immediately slide the macaroons and paper off the trays onto wire racks to cool completely.

Transfer the curd to a piping bag fitted with a 1 cm (½ inch) plain nozzle and pipe about 1 teaspoon onto half of the macaroons. Sandwich with the remaining macaroons.

CHAPTER 7:
GROWN-UP DRINKS

TEATINI

- *sugar, to rim your glasses*
- *50 ml (1 ¾ fl oz) vodka*
- *30 ml (1 fl oz) sweet iced tea*
- *10 ml (¼ fl oz) fresh lemon juice*
- *lemon wedge, to garnish*

MAKES 1

First, rim your cocktail glass or teacup with sugar and place it in the fridge to chill. Shake all the ingredients well and strain into your chilled glass. Garnish with a lemon wedge.

ENGLISH BREAKFAST

- *50 ml (1 ¾ fl oz) English Breakfast Tea infused dry gin*
- *25 ml (¾ fl oz) fresh lemon juice*
- *25 ml (¾ fl oz) pasteurized egg white (optional)*
- *7.5 ml (¼ fl oz) sugar syrup*
- *1 spoon of marmalade (about ½ tbsp)*

MAKES 1

Shake and strain into a chilled glass (either a tea cup or cocktail glass) and garnish with a zested orange peel.

THE NAUGHTY EARL

- *50 ml gin*
- *50 ml brewed and chilled Earl Grey tea*
- *squeeze of lemon juice*
- *spoonful of sugar*
- *lime wheel, to garnish*

MAKES 1

Pour all of the the ingredients into an old-fashioned glass or teacup filled with ice and stir gently. Garnish with a lime wheel.

HOT AND SPICY

- *6 tea bags or 6 rounded tsp black tea*
- *2 pieces (2 inches each) cinnamon sticks*
- *12–16 whole cloves*
- *2–3 tsp grated lemon peel*
- *220 g (7 ¾ oz/1 cup) sugar*
- *60–250 ml (2–9 fl oz/¼–1 cup) lemon juice*
- *2 pieces (2 inches each) crystallized ginger, cut lengthwise in halves*

MAKES ENOUGH FOR 10–12

Pour 3 cups boiling water to the tea. Add cinnamon sticks, cloves, and lemon peel and steep for five minutes. Remove tea bags. Add sugar and stir until dissolved, then strain. Return cinnamon sticks to the tea. Add lemon juice, 6 cups boiling water, and ginger pieces and gently stir. Serve from your favourite teapot.

AMARETTO TEA

- *180 ml (6 fl oz/¾ cup) hot black tea*
- *60 ml (2 fl oz/¼ cup) amaretto almond liqueur*
- *45 ml (1 ½ fl oz) chilled whipped cream*

MAKES 1

Pour hot tea into a teacup. Add amaretto, but do not stir. Top with cream and serve.

LE GRANDE TEA

- 1 tsp loose-leaf Golden Assam tea
- 15 ml (½ fl oz) fresh lemon juice
- 8 ml (¼ fl oz) sugar syrup
- 15 ml (½ fl oz) Benedictine
- 60 ml (2 fl oz/¼ cup) bourbon

MAKES 1

Combine tea with 250 ml (8 oz) boiling water. Let steep for about 5 minutes, then strain and refrigerate until cold. For the cocktail, shake all ingredients, except tea, with ice. Strain into ice-filled glass and top with cold tea. Gently stir to combine and garnish.

CHOCTEANI

- 15 ml (½ fl oz) dark creme de cacao
- 45 ml (1 ½ fl oz) white rum
- 120 ml (4 fl oz/½ cup) iced black tea

MAKES 1

Shake all the ingredients in a shaker with ice. Serve in a tall glass.

SOUTHERN KICK

- 15 ml (½ fl oz) whiskey
- 15 ml (½ fl oz) Southern Comfort
- 30 ml chilled black tea

MAKES 1

✳ Mix the whiskey and Southern Comfort in a teacup, and top it off with the chilled tea. Serve over ice.

OOLONG MOTEATO

- 1 heaped tbsp Oolong tea
- 2 tsp unrefined sugar
- 2–4 sprigs of fresh mint
- juice of ½ lime
- 50 ml (1 ¾ fl oz) rum

MAKES 1

* Place the tea into a teacup of hot water and allow it to infuse for one minute. Remove the leaves and allow it to cool. Muddle the sugar and mint leaves together in a shaker. Add the tea and stir until the sugar dissolves. Squeeze in the lime, add the rum and shake with ice. Strain into a teacup or cocktail glass.

THE MARTEANI

- 75 ml (2 ½ fl oz/⅓ cup) Gin
- 15 ml (½ fl oz) iced black English Breakfast Tea
- 1 milk chocolate digestive biscuit (or 2 Oreos if you're desperate)

MAKES 1

* In shaker half-filled with ice, combine gin and tea. Shake well. Strain into cocktail glass. Balance chocolate a biscuit on rim of glass to garnish.

MOROCCAN MINTEANI

* 4 whole mint leaves
* 125 ml (4 ½ fl oz/½ cup) pre-made sweetened ice tea
* splash of lime juice
* 60 ml (2 fl oz/¼ cup) vodka
* lime wedge to garnish

MAKES 1

※ Shake the mint leaves with some ice a few times. Add the remaining ingredients and shake to combine. Pour into a tall glass. Garnish with mint or a lime wedge.

BACKYARD TREAT

* 45 ml (1 ½ fl oz/¼ cup) peach puree
* ½ tbsp strong black Assam tea
* Dry lambrusco, as needed
* blackberry, for garnish

MAKES 1

※ In champagne flute, pour peach puree and tea. Do not stir. Gently fill remainder of glass with lambrusco, taking care to preserve the layers. Garnish with a blackberry

BRANDY BREAKFAST

- 60 ml (2 fl oz/¼ cup) brandy
- ½ tsp English Breakfast tea leaves
- 15 ml (½ fl oz) sugar syrup
- 1 cinnamon stick

MAKES 1

＊ Infuse the brandy with the tea leaves, and the sugar syrup with the cinnamon stick for one hour. Muddle together, then serve.

PEACH ICED TEA

950 ml (1 quart/4 cups) cold water
6 black tea bags
2 tbsp sugar
500 ml (17 fl oz/2 cups) peach nectar

whiskey
fresh peach slices, for garnish
mint sprigs, for garnish

MAKES 4

❋ Bring water to a boil in a small saucepan; remove from the heat, add tea bags, and let steep 5 minutes. Remove tea bags and stir in sugar until dissolved. Transfer to a pitcher, add peach nectar, and stir to combine. Chill in the refrigerator for at least 1 hour.

❋ Fill tall glasses with ice and then pour peach tea over, leaving some room at the top for the whiskey. Stir in 1 shot of whiskey to each glass and garnish with a peach slice and fresh mint sprig.

GREEN TEANI

35 ml (1 fl oz/⅛ cup) gin
2 slices of cucumber

60 ml (2 fl oz/¼ cup) cold green tea
juice of half a lime

MAKES 1

❋ Shake the gin, cucumber and green tea with ice. Add the lime juice and shake. Strain and serve.

INDEX

First published in 2011 by Hardie Grant Books

Hardie Grant Books (UK)
Dudley House, North Suite
34–35 Southampton Street
London WC2E 7HF
www.hardiegrant.co.uk

Hardie Grant Books (Australia)
Ground Floor, Building 1
658 Church Street
Melbourne, VIC 3121
www.hardiegrant.com.au

British Library Cataloguing-in-Publication Data. A catalogue record
for this book is available from the British Library.

ISBN 978-1-74270-194-3

Commissioning editor: Kate Pollard
Designer: Joanna Byrne
Illustrations: Emma Block
Recipe writers: Allan Campion, Michele Curtis and Deborah Kaloper
Indexer: Marian Anderson
Colour reproduction: by MDP
Printed and bound in China by 1010 Printing International Limited

10 9 8 7 6 5 4 3 2 1

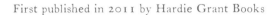